Coaching and Consulting Made Easy

"I found "Coaching and Consulting Made Easy" to be a quick and easy read, yet it was filled with great content. Chapter 3 is where the MOST useful information started flowing. I immediately applied a few of the lessons from Chapter 3 to my own business.

If you are interested in starting a coaching and consulting business...especially if you want to attract customers online or use online tools to manage and operate the business, then this is a great book to pick-up.

Even if you already have an existing coaching or consulting business, you'll pick-up a few new ideas that you can apply immediately."

- Pete Genot, Internet Marketing Coach,
PeteGenot.com

"The book is packed with 'real' tips from how to find your audience / niche to giving examples on how to price and package your services. But also everything in between and further. Brian Edmondson points you into a few directions that I felt were quite helpful. You soon understand this author knows his business and is willing to share it unlike others I read on the same subject who just used coaching formulas. What a relief not having to coach myself again!!!"

- Christina Bucher, Goal-Clarity.com

"If you're just getting started with coaching or have been wondering what it takes to be a coach - this is the book for you! It is all inclusive with what you need to know to get started."

- Shari McGuire, Shrink Your Work Week

"[This] is a great book for anyone with expertise in something -- anything, really. Brian's book makes it easy to start your own business helping people and making money while doing it. This book is easy to read, with tons of great advice from one of the great minds and coaches in marketing. Seriously, this book is a MUST read, even if you're only considering coaching and/or consulting now or in the future. Brian will definitely get you going in the right direction.

- Pat Marcello, MagnaSites.com

"This book can help you make a decision about whether or not business or life coaching is for you. If you decide it is, it's a wonderful and easy-to-read book about how to get started."

- James Hubbard, Tupelo, MS USA

Coaching & Consulting Made Easy

COACHING
& CONSULTING
MADE EASY

HOW TO START, BUILD, AND GROW A
PROFIT-PULLING COACHING & CONSULTING BUSINESS
BY TURNING YOUR KNOWLEDGE INTO MONEY!

BRIAN T. EDMONDSON
InternetIncomeCoach.com

Dedication

This book is dedicated to all the past, present, and future coaches who have dedicated their lives to helping others improve their lives.

The world is a better place because of you.

CONTENTS

Free "Internet Profit Report" Bonus Report

I'd like to personally thank you for investing in Coaching and Consulting Made Easy: How to Start, Build, and Grow a Profit-Pulling Coaching & Consulting Business by Turning Your Knowledge Into Money!

As a special unadvertised bonus for purchasing Coaching and Consulting Made Easy, I put together a special "Internet Profit Report" that reveals exactly how I use the internet to get traffic to my websites, build an audience, and get sales.

You can download your free bonus report right now at:

http://internetincomecoach.com

Enjoy the free report, and go ahead and dive into the rest of this book. You'll find the information straightforward, fun, and easy to read. To your coaching and consulting success!

Sincerely,

Brian T. Edmondson
InternetIncomeCoach.com

Chapter 1

Is a Coaching Business Right for You?

There's a specific business model that many professionals are pursuing to cash in on their expertise. It's commonly known as coaching or consulting, and it's gone to a whole new level of profitability thanks to the Internet.

Whether you've been an experienced coach offline and want to take your business onto the World Wide Web, or you've never had experience as an official coach, you'll have a formidable action plan by the end of this book that can show you how to turn a profit helping others improve their lives.

Not only will you be able to enjoy tremendous financial gains from your efforts – because the coaching business is booming – but you'll also enjoy the personal satisfaction that goes along with it.

The wonderful thing about creating a coaching business online is that it allows you to reach a global audience – and create a specific business model unlike any other.

You can't come across as someone desperate to get a client base – because who wants to receive coaching from someone who is struggling themselves? You have to learn how to project success and competence.

You can't just say, "I coach people," whenever someone asks you what you do. You want to create a plan where you have a specific answer, such as, "I help executives increase their company's bottom line by 20% or more." Or, "I help women get past the pain of divorce."

Once you know who you want to target, you'll be developing a plan that helps you land and keep those clients on your roster.

Who Is Right for a Coaching Business?

Coaching is the right business model for people who take pleasure out of helping others achieve success or goals. Authors, coaches, speakers, and those with a passion for helping people overcome obstacles do really well with coaching – when they have the right business model to pursue.

It's a sad fact that most men and women who enter coaching end up failing with it financially. That's because coaching is just as much about the business aspect as it is helping people. You're running a bona fide business, so you have to be open to learning about marketing, promotion, client attraction and retention, and more.

Once you see this as an on-going education for yourself, something you strive to better over time, you'll get to a point where not only is your client roster full (overflowing), but you're commanding more money for each coaching appointment they schedule.

It's simply not enough to undergo coaching training on *how* to coach – you have to be skilled at building a thriving practice or all the training in the world won't help. The type of person who does well as a coach also has the basics of coaching mastered. That includes things like:

- Having patience with people as they grow out of a problem.

- Listening to their needs and providing solutions on the fly.

- Possessing the ability to look past their "stories" and help them achieve clarity on issues.

- Communicating well with different types of people, making them feel comfortable and safe during the process.

What Kind of Coaching Can You Do Online?

There are two basic categories for coaches to pursue; business coaching and life / personal coaching. You can certainly overlap, though it might be better to become known as a niche authority figure for one particular target audience.

Both coaches are being hired to help the people get results. Your clients want to know ahead of time what you can help them achieve – in measurable terms. Whether it's weight loss, months until their relationship improves, or financial goals – you have to be able to deliver.

Business coaches are the ones who help people achieve career dreams, meet financial goals, and generally climb the ladder to where they want to be. You can coach individuals or companies as a whole.

Sometimes, companies will bring on a coach to help work with their individual employees – that's a very lucrative arrangement that can instantly book your schedule for a long time.

Life coaches are the other type of option – and they specifically work with individuals on self-improvement and personal development issues. It might be sheer happiness, or something specific, like getting rid of food guilt or abandonment issues.

Let's go over both types of coaching and see if it helps you decide which one you want to pursue, starting with personal coaching. Some coaches work with people on a wide range of issues – increasing energy, finding true love, achieving happiness, you name it.

But you can also be a coach for a specific target audience if you want to – like a spiritual coach or relationship coach for couples or individuals. You should write down the various issues you enjoy helping people with – topics you feel qualified to assist in as a neutral party.

There are many positive aspects of being a personal coach. The great thing about it is that you have the opportunity to work with a wide range of people – and this diversity is an attractive option to many coaches.

There's a never-ending audience of individuals who need this type of coaching, too. Every age group, both genders, and those with all types of problems seek personal coaches to help guide them past obstacles in their lives.

There are also some things you may not enjoy about personal coaching. For example, some clients can become dependent on you to the point of needing you to rescue them from a crisis all the time.

Another problem is that if you don't focus your practice on one target audience, then you might feel lost in a sea of competition due to the sheer magnitude of the marketplace.

Personal coaching isn't as lucrative as business coaching, assuming your client roster is filled with each example. That's because individuals find it harder to invest in themselves – whereas a company looks at the investment as a potential for growth and prosperity. They expect to get a return on their investment, whereas an individual is wary that it may not happen.

With business coaching, the person or team who hires you will be looking for you to achieve results like increasing morale, upping productivity and performance, and helping motivate and inspire employees to achieve their goals, which in turn helps the company raise their bottom line.

They might have you also help employees get more organized, plan more effectively, and communicate better. Many companies will enlist your help with creating team-building exercises, too.

You may have thought you wanted to help individuals with personal career coaching – and you may still. But it's exciting to help a company develop an entire team that rises to new levels of achievement, too.

You can tailor your practice to helping teams, low-level workers, or top executives in a company. The higher the level, the more you have to bring to the table in terms of qualifications and abilities.

Companies will hire you to do things like transition new leadership in and out of a business, develop a training program, and mediate problems that arise between co-workers.

There's going to be tougher competition when it comes to getting a business account. The research team won't just hire the first person who contacts them – they'll scout out a bunch of coaches and have them compete for the business, or measure up better than the competition.

Most of the work you'll be doing for a business will be to fix a problem. When things are going well, a coach typically isn't sought out for the workplace. So expect to go into a situation that's volatile and unsteady.

You'll want to have a plan to help rescue the company from whatever is affecting them, and then present a reason for them to keep you on hand for an even bigger perk of increasing profits and performance.

As a business coach, you might be asked about your understanding of how a business operates – things like leadership and sales skills, aspects of management, and the language of the corporate world. You'll have to be educated about the organization of a corporation or company like the hierarchy of positions.

They'll be looking to see how you communicate and interact with others. If you have previous experience in the business world yourself, this will be a perk because you're an insider.

Whichever path you pursue – business or personal – focus your efforts of attracting clients who have it in them to succeed. You shouldn't be promoting yourself the same way a psychologist would – someone who can help with deeper mental issues.

Your goal is to provide guidance for a better life, not to rescue someone from an emotional sinkhole that will be hard to climb out of without medical intervention. This will also enable you to have a higher success rate with your clients.

How the Internet Works With Online Coaching

You might have a thriving or new offline coaching business where you want to attract local clients into your office. If that's the case, then you'll simply need to create a presence online and position it to target your local client base.

That will include setting yourself up to attract traffic for prospective clients who go online and type things into Google like this: "Life Coach Seattle" or "Executive Coach Dallas, Texas."

But many coaches are turning the Internet into their actual place of business. Not only do they use it to get found by potential clients, but they also cater to them over the World Wide Web. You can work one-on-one with people or work with groups.

They use a variety of tools and strategies to accomplish this – things like Skype, Webinars, ecourses, and membership areas. We'll get into all of this later in the book – but just know that using the Internet open up an entirely new world of profit potential for you.

Having an Unofficial Business Plan in Place

Starting an Internet-based coaching business doesn't require a significant amount of monetary investment up front - or at any later date for that matter. But you still want to create a plan of sorts to ensure that you're staying on the right track as you launch and grow your business.

You just want to make sure that you've thought this through, that you have a good idea of how it will work, and that you're ready to move forward. You don't need to write an official business plan that you would normally share with a financial advisor or bank representative. This will be different.

First, ask yourself if you believe you will thoroughly enjoy launching a business or personal coaching company. Will you be able to handle the entire task list that includes market research, marketing, client acquisition and retention, and more? Or were you just hoping to hang your shingle and have needy people flood into your website looking for help?

Write down a clear statement about what your target audience is. Get as in-depth as you want. We'll go into more detail on your target audience in the next chapter, but for now, have an idea and describe that audience.

Develop a statement of how you help that specific group of individuals. What strategies do you use, what measurements do you take to foster the kind of results you hope to achieve?

Add to your business plan the kinds of services and products you hope to develop and offer over time. This can change as your business grows. You might start with services and eventually add products to your roster.

Have some of your own goals that you plan to achieve – both monetary and growth-wise. Do you want to make six figures by year two? Have a certain number of clients on your list? Write it down so that you can refer to it and pursue these objectives as you plan and implement your strategy.

Who will your competition be? Look online and in your local area, if you're also working offline, and write down your top 10 competitors. Do a little analysis of what their business entails because you'll want to do yours better.

It's not just official online business and personal life coaches who are your competition, either. Think of anything or anyone that could take away business from you. That could include:

- Other coaches targeting the same niche audience

- Professional organizations that offer similar coaching programs

- Seminars and conferences held on the topics you specialize in (like time management)

- Economic downturn (since coaching would be one of the first luxuries to be cut if a company had to watch its budget closer)

- Other online and offline courses – including books, eBooks, video and audio presentations, not to mention membership sites

How will you position yourself in the marketplace to be a better option than those competitors? You have to have something unique that sets you apart – some sort of advantage your client gets for hiring you instead of someone else.

Look at the competition in terms of their rates, their offerings, their promises, their past client roster (if listed), how they market to the public to attract clients, and what gap you see in the marketplace that they're not addressing.

How will you market your business? You're going to learn about that in the remainder of this book. But be prepared to add your options to your unofficial business plan so that you'll be ready to implement and tweak it as you go.

In addition to the start-up costs you need, even if minimal, write down what you project for your earnings over the first through fourth quarter of the coming year. Keep a profit and loss statement so that you know where all of your incoming and outgoing funds are from.

Now that you have a good overview of what it takes to launch and grow a thriving coaching business online, let's take a look at how you zero in on your target audience. Once you're able to profile them well, it will be easy to market to their needs.

Chapter 2

Honing in on Your Target Audience

Before you begin marketing to anyone for your coaching services, you have to have an image of them in mind – a profile that tells you what their needs are, what their objections may be, and what they're hoping to achieve if they hire you.

Knowing all of this allows you to present yourself in a way that has them absolutely convinced you're the right person for the job.

Zero in on a Specific Group of Customers

As mentioned in the last chapter, it is possible to offer a one size fits all broad-based coaching business. But you're going to find that your success soars when you become a specialty coach – providing services for one core niche group.

Have you ever heard the phrase, "jack of all trades, and master of none?" That's what happens when you try to serve *everyone* – no one thinks that you're a master of one type of coaching.

Think about it in personal terms. If you were having extreme foot pain, would you prefer to see your general practitioner or would you prefer to see a podiatrist who specializes in feet?

In terms of coaching, if you were having relationship troubles, and wanted to save your marriage, would you prefer to see a general life coach or a relationship coach?

Specializing in one core niche audience is not only smart when it comes to being able to tailor your marketing message, but it also lessens the chaos for you as a coach, and helps you develop your skills in one area, rather than you having to be all over the place with your training.

How to Profile the Kind of People You Want to Coach

You can start by creating a customer profile that helps you categorize your prospective customers in a simple way. These categories may or may not be integrated into your marketing campaign, but they will be reflected in your message in some way.

Some of them you may not find relevant. For example, age will be one factor – and that might apply to your coaching or not. For example, you might be a career coach who helps middle aged and senior employees switch to a new career, or level up in their existing one. Or maybe you're a personal life coach for teens ages 13-18.

Pick whichever categories help you promote your business and feel free to leave the ones that don't apply.

There are eight basic categories:

Age

Age is a self-explanatory one. You will want to write down a range of ages, though. You can do it like our example above, where you tackle specific ranges (13-18, 25-35, 40-60, etc.)

Or, you can do it in a more generic manner, like this: teens, young adults, middle-aged men and women, senior citizens. Either way is acceptable, but the more specific you can be, the better your marketing will evolve.

Sex

Which gender, if either, do you feel more comfortable coaching? You can certainly coach both men and women, but depending on what niche you choose, you might have a preference.

Over time, you might have a percentage that you notice – like 30% women, and 70% men. If that's the case, then you may end up tweaking your marketing message to either cater to the male audience or do a better job in attracting the female customers.

Race

There are some coaches who work with a specific ethnicity. You might target Hispanics or African Americans for a specific reason. For example, maybe you're a business and life coach for African American women in the workforce.

Location

This will usually only play a role if you're using your coaching business offline. On the Internet, you can typically create a global angle – but you might want to focus on Americans or citizens of whatever country you happen to live in.

This might make a difference online if you don't know the cultures and business climate of the other nations. Otherwise, it won't have any relevance and you can leave it off of your profile list.

Education

This is very important in terms of career. There will be people who lack a college degree who go to a coach to help them learn how to enhance their employability in the workforce.

There will also be people with a college degree who want to achieve the greatest success they can, but they're confused about how to apply that education to finding the right job.

Industry or Career

You might find that you want to focus on one level or type of business. So your profile might include things like "law professionals" or "computer industry." It might also include "human resources" or "executives."

These trigger words show the industry and the level of success or departments within a workplace that you're best at working with.

Income and Profits

Another important business coaching category, the finances play an important role because while some people will seek your help in assisting them in finding personal satisfaction on the job, many will be concerned about upping the ante in terms of salary.

You might want to profile workers who are already at a six-figure level of success. Or maybe you take on clients who *want* to get there, but who haven't reached it yet — and that becomes your promise of results.

In terms of coaching at companies, they may want you to prove that you can handle helping them increase the financial objectives of the business. So you might target Forbes 500 companies for example, or start-up businesses!

Goals

Goals that your prospective clients have can be personal or professional. Professionally, maybe they are looking for a career that keeps them feeling challenged and engaged in new adventures.

Or perhaps they worry about job security in an unstable market and they need you to help them develop traits that make employers want to retain them on staff. These are career goals that you can help them achieve.

With personal coaching, you might have clients whose goals are to find a satisfying relationship — or be happy on their own. Maybe they want to improve their time management skills so that they have a better work-life balance.

You don't have to focus on *just* one profile. You can have a back-up or secondary ideal customer in mind. For example, your primary customer might be six figure salaried employees – and your secondary one can be those not quite to that level yet.

Business Coaching Audiences

When you're pursing life coaching with individuals – it may or may not have to do with their professional goals. It might relate to their weight, their relationships, their energy levels or other issues.

But when you become a business coach, you're 100% immersed in career topics. So I want to take a moment to show you how you can break this category down even further – because the competition will be stiffer and the more qualified and targeted you are, the more success you'll see.

Above, we talked about categorizing prospective clients based on things like age, gender, race, location and goals. With business coaching, you can break it down into other areas you want to pursue.

Top Industries That Use Coaching

The first consideration you should make when targeting an audience according to industry is whether or not you have experience in that profession yourself. If so, an insider's point of view is always appreciated and can help you edge out the competition.

Service providers like lawyers, medical professionals, technicians and other areas often seek out coaching to help grow their practice or business into something formidable in the marketplace.

They need help positioning themselves in the market, increasing earnings, dealing with conflict and recruiting people for their agency or firm. You can look for industries that use coaching services online.

Using various tools that show which phrases people are searching on Google for, you might see that these industries are seeking out business coaching: construction, accounting, art, actors, doctors, interior designers, personal trainers, photographers, realtors, beauty salons, therapists, and more.

Positions That Often Seek Out Coaches

As we'll go into in depth later, you might be brought on to work with a team of professionals – like motivating and coaching a sales team to deliver a higher profit margin for the company.

With a team, they'll rely on your improve morale, conduct conflict resolution, come up with training improvements, and assist with communication. You won't be able to work one-on-one but will *have* to work in groups in most instances.

Coaches might be brought in to work with management – either individually or as a group. Companies want you to help them learn how to inspire their staff and communicate well. They should focus on team-building skills, too.

If the person is new to management, then you'll want to have a specific program designed to hone their skills in handling a group of people below them on the ladder of success.

If they're not new, but you're being brought in to work with a manager, then it usually means there's a problem they want you to help resolve. It could be something that lower level employees have complained about, like inappropriate behavior or anger.

It doesn't always mean that, though. Sometimes you're brought in to help transition people from one department or position to another. Maybe a mid-level manager is being bumped up to executive and they want him to be able to handle the responsibilities.

Individual Versus Group Career Coaching

In later chapters we'll dig down into the personal versus group coaching options, but let's talk about what companies actually hire you for in terms of the size of the groups you'll have an opportunity to work with.

Let's start with the solo entrepreneur or small business owner. This is someone who has launched his or her own business and is seeking your coaching to help them get to a higher level of success.

This type of client is a hard worker who shows initiative in building a business and taking risks. If they seek you out, you'll know they're serious in investing in themselves and will implement your advice.

They're typically after help with time management and focus because they have to wear many hats at once to build their business, even if they have a small staff of helpers.

There can be drawbacks to working with a motivated entrepreneur. Some might try to offer you a deal where you get a cut of their profits instead of money upfront. And because it's just one person, or a few, it can be a shortened engagement because once you help them master their issue, they won't need you anymore.

You'll generally find these kinds of clients when they're in a transition stage in their lives. Maybe they were laid off by a larger company and branched out to build their own business for security reasons.

It's important that you understand the fundamentals of running a business because they'll often be lost and confused about how it all works together. Someone who is a skilled technical like a computer consultant or electrician might be great at their craft, but have no clue how to run a business.

They may feel uneasy about certain aspects of their new business – like getting out there and marketing their services. You can help them with that by teaching them how to communicate better with their target audience.

You'll need to pace the process in how hard and how fast you push them out of their comfort zone. They will already be mired in confusion of running a business, so focus on what their immediate needs are that will deliver the best results for them and show them that you're worth their investment.

That might be time management skills – helping them map out a plan and implement it in the best way possible so that there's ample time If they're operating a small business, then maybe their problem will be managing employees and making the most of their resources.

Entrepreneurs often have a hard time delegating tasks to someone else. They're typically people who know the way they want to get things done, and don't want to risk having someone else come onboard who will "mess things up" by doing it a different way.

For these individuals and small businesses, the major issues they'll bring you on for include improving sales, growth, leadership and management, customer service communication, conflict and acquiring a good staff. For an individual, they may need help with outsourcing rather than an in-house staff.

A middle-sized company – in between an entrepreneur or small business and a large corporation – often has a different set of needs. They're always in a constant state of growth, so they need a coach for transition teams.

They are looking for someone to help them recruit the very best their industry has to offer in terms of talent. They need training advice for new hires. They want a coach who knows what technology might help them advance *more*, faster.

They may have more people to share the duties, but that also creates a different kind of chaos. They suddenly have a swollen employee roster and need help learning how to manage all of the various personalities, talents and tasks.

It's at this level where a company might need coaching advice for inter-departmental issues. Problems can arise when groups within a business are split off into sectors, instead of one cohesive unit.

The great thing is, middle-sized companies are in the position where they are striving to grow even more, and worried about slipping backward among a sea of competitors.

The bad news is, it becomes harder for the various department heads and gatekeepers within the company to make a unanimous decision to bring in outside help in the form of coaching because there is now allocated funding for each area within the company and your payment has to come from somewhere.

Large companies and corporations are the big fish in the pond — the hardest gigs to land — but the most lucrative. Once you land one of these it will be much easier for you to accumulate a profitable client list.

You might find that this turns into a long-term, all-encompassing gig for you. You can be brought in for one department and be utilized after the completion of those goals in many other departments.

Large companies are willing to pay hefty sums – but they want impressive (and measurable) results. If you find a company with an open mind to what you bring to the table, then you'll have the ability to make a strong impact.

If you encounter a corporation with strict ways of doing things, and an unwillingness to actually incorporate your changes, then you might struggle to prove your worth – even if it's at their own fault.

The process to get hired on for a job isn't fast – it's often lengthy and complex. You'll need to submit proposals, meet with decision makers, and wait for project approval.

Payment takes awhile, too. There's not an entrepreneur or accountant waiting to cut you a check. The payment has to be submitted and approved and then released over a longer timespan. Vendors typically wait 30-120 days for payment from corporations, so expect a wait – but know that it can be well worth it.

To land a large company's coaching gig, you may have to bring other coaches onboard with you. Groups tend to do better than individuals because of the sheer size of the company.

Are You Qualified to Coach Them With Their Needs?

Once you've created a prospective customer profile, you'll be able to work on your marketing materials as well as your skills in providing the best services to them.

You can't just wake up one day and launch a coaching business where you help transition executive leadership in and out of a corporation. You have to have an understanding about how the process works and what all is involved.

You have to be able to speak the language of a corporation and grasp the wording that's used in the company in terms of positions, goals, and more. For example, you would need to know P&L and ROI.

If you already have ample experience because you've been through the process before, then that's great! You have hands-on qualifications. There will be some continuing education involved if you have no experience – and you'll have to prove your worth and understanding more than someone will a hefty portfolio of previous success stories.

Even with personal coaching, your clients will want to know (and you'll want to convey in your marketing message) what qualifications you have in helping them deal with their goals.

If it's the weight loss niche, then you will have a hard time coaching others if you're extremely overweight yourself. Your credibility will suffer because they want to see that you're capable of implementing your own advice.

If you're coaching couples through bad relationships, and you've been divorced five times, then that won't be a strong selling point – and it might show *you* that you need to get coaching on that topic yourself – and you may not be qualified to help others.

Now in some instances, your own past experience will come in handy. A former drug addict who can coach existing drug addicts about how to get sober and stay clean is a wonderful thing – because you *have* achieved the goal they themselves are hoping to mimic.

Start looking to see where you need to get a better education or more experience for the target audience that you just mapped out and then work that into your business plan as an on-going task.

Do You Enjoy That Niche Group?

The best way to succeed in any career is to really enjoy it and to have a passion for it. Don't launch a coaching business based strictly on research and volume of potential clients.

Instead, look at how you would feel in terms of personal satisfaction when it comes to working with a specific group of people. If you really enjoy working with young adults instead of seniors, then target the group you want.

If you're not sure if you would enjoy coaching a particular group in a category listing, then spend some time interacting with that target market. Get to know them as people and see how you *feel* when you're engaged with them in a non-coaching situation.

You might even offer a few free coaching sessions to see how you are able to assist that specific group with their needs – *and* how you feel being immersed in that category day in, day out.

When you're truly satisfied with a demographic, you'll crave the ability to add value to their coaching sessions. It will make you a better guide because you'll seek out ways to help them – information and tools you can use in your arsenal to help them overcome their obstacles.

Once you narrow down your niche audience, it will be time to get ready to go through the launch process. You want to have a plan in place – action steps you can take to garner interest in your services and achieve great success!

Chapter 3

Launching Your Coaching Business Online

Once you've determined what kind of coaching you want to pursue, and you've narrowed down a target audience, it will be time for you to take the next step forward in building your business online.

This is the time when you start getting set up with a home on the World Wide Web, figuring out how you'll appeal to prospective clients, and begin branding yourself the way you want to be known.

Traditional Versus Online Business Start Up Needs

Some people balk when they're told they have any sort of investment, but whether you're online or offline, you will need a little bit of start-up money to get the ball rolling.

The main difference is in *how much* money you'll need. With an offline coaching business, you have to think about office space, office furniture, equipment, possibly a secretary, and more.

Online – it's not like that at all. You have a virtual office. Now that doesn't mean you can't have funds set aside for office space in your home – or even go ahead and rent office space elsewhere if you prefer to – but it's not a necessity.

Offline, you're going to have to pay for more advertising and marketing – and a little cash does not go a long way in terms of strategically reaching your core audience.

But online, it's cheap, if not free, to reach a wide audience interested in your products and services – and it operates 24/7, 365 days a year. You're really getting a lot for your investment of time (and sometimes a little bit of money).

There are a few online startup costs, though. You'll need to set aside a little money for things like:

- Domain URL

- Hosting account

- Computer with web cam and headsets

- Meeting tools

- Marketing costs (like website graphics, paid ad campaigns, etc.)

But there are always free ways to do most things if you're on a very tight budget. For example, we're going to cover some paid tools that let you meet with clients – but there's always Skype, which is a free download option you can use to video or audio chat with them.

A Domain and Hosting Serve as Your Online Office

If you're new to the Internet (at least as a business or more than catching up with friends and family on Facebook), don't worry – it's not difficult and not nearly as expensive as some people would have you believe.

A domain name will be the URL address that people go to when they want to find out about your products and services – and about *you*. Domain names cost around $10 (cheaper if you find a coupon code for the domain seller) for an entire *year*.

You have some choices on what kind of domain name you want. First, consider the extension you'll be using. It's always best to go with a dot com (.com) website.

It's the one most people instinctively type in when they're searching for something – so try to avoid dot net, dot info, or dot org sites. Dot com sites are more expensive than others (for instance, a dot com might be $10/year while a dot info domain is $2/year) but they're worth it because you're catering to a consumer's habit of typing dot com.

The next thing you want to consider is what your domain name will be. You have a few choices – play around with it. Consider these variations:

JaneDoe.com would be a great domain (replacing Jane Doe with your own name, of course) because it brands you specifically – and many people do well with this type of branding, such as Tony Robbins.

Another option – if your name happens to be taken, would be to use a middle initial with it – or, simply put something like this: JaneDoeCoaching.com. You could also turn it around and use: CoachJaneDoe.com.

But what if you prefer to brand a business name instead of your own personal name? That's fine, too! You might name your business Executive Coaching Center – and you can stick a dot com on the end of that and you're good to go.

The best way to create a business name and domain if you're not using your personal name is to ensure that the potential client recognizes what your business is all about.

With our example of Executive Business Coaching, that's pretty straightforward as to what it's about. Here are some other examples:

- Relationship Couples Coaching

- College Graduate Job Coach

- Energy Healing Coaching

- Teen Life Coach

- Hispanic Women Career Coach

See how narrowed and specific that is? Just upon seeing your domain name – and nothing else – the prospective client instantly knows what kind of coaching you offer.

Where should you get a domain name? There are many companies to choose from. One of the most popular ones is called GoDaddy – and you can usually find coupon codes that knock off some of the cost.

Once you purchase a domain (and don't worry about accepting all of the various add-on products and services they offer throughout the checkout process), you'll need to get a hosting account.

There are many hosting providers to choose from. One popular one that offers 24/7 help via chat or phone is called HostGator. Regardless of which company you choose, you'll be given a login area known as your cpanel.

This is where you'll go to upload files for your website graphics, blog, and even your products. A host is the service that keeps your website live to the public – so you want a host that has good "up time," which means your website is live almost 100% of the time without disruption.

You don't need a huge account at first. Over time, you might want to branch out and create separate websites for individual types of coaching or products, but initially, all you need is enough hosting to service a single website.

Once you have hosting, you can set up an email address for your domain so that when a visitor lands on your site and wants to contact you, they can email you at a professional contact address – like Jane@JanceDoeCoaching.com for example.

Website Setup

The easiest way to set up a coaching website is to install a blog on your domain. Blogs are well-liked by Google and other search engines – and it gives you a way to have a home for showcasing your products and services *and* to attract visitors who might be interested in your coaching with your valuable content.

Installing a blog is very simple – since your host will probably have a convenient Fantastico button in your cpanel that helps you click, fill in a few blank areas, and create a blog.

But if you prefer not to have a blog, you can go to the extra effort of creating a static website. There are many tools you can invest in to learn how to do this yourself, like DreamWeaver, or you can hire someone to create a website for you.

Graphics will be important for your website. You can certainly go the do it yourself route, but just be aware that unless you have ample experience with graphic creation, they're likely to come across as amateurish.

You can find a graphic creator online who can create:

- Blog themes

- Website header, footer and background

- eBook covers (for your products that you create)

- Banner ads (if you want to pay for traffic from other sites)

...and more.

Pages that you'll want to include on your coaching site may include:

Home Page

The home page will be a short, introductory message welcoming your visitors and summing up what it is you can do for them. You want to focus more on the benefits you can offer them than you focus on details about yourself on this main page.

You can also have an opt in form on this page. We'll talk about this more in Chapter 5, but you can create a system that captures a visitor's name and email address and allows you to contact them in the future and hopefully convert them into buyers.

About Page

An About page is where the prospective client gets to find out about you. Make sure you have a picture of yourself and a friendly message that describes who you are, your background, educational accomplishments – and anything else you feel is relevant for them to determine whether or not you're a good fit for them and vice versa.

Service Page

A Service page is where you can list all of the services you have available to your prospective clients. You might include package deals (which we'll cover later), group sessions, and more.

Some coaches will have an order button right on their site where the client can purchase a service and check out. Others like to have an initial conversation with prospective clients to determine whether or not it's an ideal pairing.

Product Page

A product page will be where your eCover graphics represent the content that you're selling. Coaching (Tony Robbins is a good example), put out all sorts of products, such as eBooks, video courses, podcasts, and membership programs.

This is a good page to have – even if you only offer services right now. You can sign up to be an affiliate (where you earn a commission for recommending other people's products) and post links and short reviews to relevant products you feel your service-based customers might benefit from.

Testimonial Page

A testimonial page might be bare at first, but as you have loyal customers returning to get coaching from you, this will fill up and help convince other prospective clients to give your services a try.

Branding Your Coaching Business Online

When you start branding yourself online, you want to focus on what you can do for others, not your resume or what courses you've taken that had a profound impact on you.

If you have results to talk about, then that's certainly relevant for people to know. But your branding will be mostly about how you want to be known. Try filling in this statement:

Jane Doe is the coach who _____.

What would you like people to say about you? You're the coach who gets people to seven figure incomes? You're the coach who fixes even the most hopeless marriages?

Think of a brand and then build it for yourself online by promoting yourself as THE go to person for your target audience.

Have a tag line for your website that sums it all up for them. A tag line is like a motto – a short phrase or sentence that lets the visitor know what your site is about. It has to be pretty specific – not just "helping people."

So let's look at possible tag lines for a couple of our previous domain examples:

- EnergyHealingCoaching.com – *Refocusing Anxiety Into Positive Progress*

- TeenLifeCoach.com – *Helping Teens Cope With Stressful Situations*

By using a tag line, it helps the visitor know what direction or specialty you have in your coaching business. TeenLifeCoach.com, for example, could be coaching teens for their future careers, coaching them through addictive behaviors, or many other issues.

EnergyHealingCoaching.com might be a domain that helps people get over medical or physical obstacles using energy healing or it could be to help people get over stress or depression.

A tag line can help pinpoint your branding message. Spend some time working on your motto and playing with words and adjectives that reflect the purpose you have for your site.

Get Your Marketing Message Out to the Paying Public

Your marketing message is slightly different from your branding. With branding, the focus is on how you want to be known to the target audience. It's what adjective you want your name to be synonymous with.

With marketing, you're creating a message that speaks to the needs of the prospective client. It's expanding on your tagline that you created with your branding efforts.

We're going to focus on marketing online, but don't forget that you can have business cards, flyers or brochures created for offline usage that directs people to your online website.

We'll go over various ways to attract and generate traffic to your website later, but for now, let's focus on how you want to market to a particular group of potential customers.

For personal coaching, you want a heavy focus on whatever area of life that you offer help with. If it's relationships, for example, then make sure your marketing materials speaks to how the client is feeling.

Here are some examples of what a person or couple in the midst of relationship troubles might be feeling:

- Sad

- Angry

- Depressed

- Hopeless

- Worried

- Frustrated

Make sure you address that in your marketing – and how you can help them overcome those feelings. People will come to you looking for solutions – to *feel* better in terms of personal coaching.

Business coaching is a bit different. They want measurable results. You have to present yourself as a true professional with a list of credentials and proven results to land big clients.

Testimonials and references will play a big role in your marketing materials. Anytime you can name drop, that's a good addition to your marketing materials. If your client is willing to be contacted as a reference, that's even better.

Marketing materials for business coaches should use facts and figures — such as "...helped the company increase their ROI by 25% in 60 days." Or, you might say something like, "Clients typically see a 20% increase in their salary within the first six months."

Think about what your prospective business client needs: more time, more money, more confidence, and more skills. How can you convey that you'll help them achieve these goals through your coaching?

If you go into business coaching with the intention of focusing on one specific area, make sure you reflect that in your marketing materials. For example, instead of calling yourself a "business coach," make sure you specify if you're specifically geared to help with transitions or customer service management.

If you're preparing marketing materials for a specific company, then do some diligent research on the history and background and current operations of the company.

You'll want your materials to accurately reflect their needs – not a broad overview of businesses in general. Look at trends in their industry and try to speak about how you can help them compete in the marketplace.

Don't create your marketing materials to attract the low-level employees if it's the higher-ups that will be making the decisions about whether or not to hire you. You want to speak the right language and offer the right solutions.

If you're offering training to a company's employees, then make sure you research what they're already doing to train them – so that you don't duplicate what's being done, but complement or improve it.

Marketing materials offline consist of text, radio and television ads. Online, you can mix audio and video usage with text, too – only it won't cost an arm and a leg like it does offline.

Online, consumers are used to YouTube and podcasts – so they often prefer that type of message to a text-based one. You'll want to cater to everyone, so make sure you have a mix.

You can have a text-based welcome (or home) page on your site, and add a video message on your About page so that clients can get to know you better. You can use a podcast service on a service like iTunes (free) to deliver a message to your loyal followers.

Tools That Allow You to "Meet" With Clients

Before your launch, you need to have tools in place that allow you to meet with your clients in a virtual setting. Gone are the days when a landline phone was your only option.

We're going to cover two options – a paid and a free tool that will allow you to talk to individuals or groups, depending on what type of coaching you want to offer.

Free is always good if you're starting out on a budget. It's not always the most professional option – or the one that provides access to the most perks – but it's available if needed.

If you're just starting your coaching business and need to stick within a tight budget, then you might want to consider using Skype. Skype is free and easy to download and set up in a flash.

You'll have your client download the tool, too – and both of you can talk for an unlimited time with no cost – and it's global! (Although as a coach, you'll want to have a set time for the call to last).

With Skype, you can have a chat with your client in one of three ways:

- Text, which is just like an instant messenger where you type back and forth.

- Audio, which is where you chat like you would over a phone line.

- Video, which allows you to work with your client in a visual, face-to-face manner.

The choice is up to you – and you may want to give your clients a choice, depending on what they feel most comfortable with, too.

You can also share files over the Skype service. This will be perfect for whenever you have an array of products or tools that you provide to your client to help them achieve their goals.

There is a paid version of the service that allows you to do group video coaching calls for up to 10 people and voice only calls for up to 25 people.

You can also do screen sharing for free, which is where you allow the client you're coaching to see your computer screen. This might be perfect if you want to present a PowerPoint presentation, for example. For groups, you can do screen sharing if you have the premium version of Skype.

One benefit you can provide to your coaching clients is a recorded version of their coaching session. This is something you can do on Skype, too, although the recording service isn't built in – you have to find a separate tool to help you do that.

How much is the premium feature of Skype? It starts at just $4.99 a month if you invest in a year subscription. If you decide to go month-to-month instead, then the price increases to $9.99 a month, but that's still very affordable – much less than renting office space locally!

Now let's look at a paid tool that lets you hold meetings or webinars with your clients – they're part of the "Go To" suite of products – GoToMeeting, GoToWebinar, and GoToTraining.

GoToMeeting has a free 30-day trial before you buy it. You can host a meeting for up to 25 people and share your screen with them or have a face-to-face conference.

The people who attend your meeting can use their computer or an iPhone or iPad – even an Android works for this program. It has a built in system to record the meeting, so you can share it afterwards with those who attended, or use it to improve on your coaching.

You can allow other people to be presenters on the coaching call, if you bring in another expert. Plus, you can draw on the screen to make it more interactive if you're doing some sort of training session that needs further explanation.

GoToMeeting is $49 per month or $468 for a year subscription, which helps you save 20%. You get unlimited use of the product when you sign up. But there are two other options that *include* GoToMeeting – so let's look at the next one.

GoToWebinar is perfect for those of you who plan to go after medium to large size businesses. It allows you to host a webinar with up to 1,000 attendees. This eliminates the need for you to be on-site. You can record the presentation for later use.

The quality of the video is very high — broadcast in HD. You simply schedule the webinar, invite the people to attend, and start it when ready! One really cool part of the Webinar tool is that it gives you some analysis afterwards.

You can click "Generate Reports" and get details about how many people attended the webinar, how engaged they were with you during the event, and even survey them on their satisfaction.

Engaged audience participation is achieved through the use of built-in polling abilities, Q&A options, and the attendees' ability to "raise their hand" during the event.

GoToWebinar also has a 30-day free trial, and it includes GoToMeeting when you purchase it. It's priced according to audience size. It breaks down like this:

- Up to 100 people is $99 a month or $948 a year.

- Up to 500 people is $399 a month or $3,828 a year.

- Up to 1,000 people is $499 a month or $4,788 a year.

The last option is GoToTraining. Again, they have a free 30-day trial. This is for up to 200 attendees and it's a tool geared toward a class where you can test the attendees poll them, and generate class evaluations.

You can actually charge the people attending this coaching session – it's all built into the system and you can offer a flexible payment plan. You can create a catalog of classes that you offer.

GoToTraining has two different pricing plans. With both, you get GoToMeeting for free. The first one provides up to 25 people for $149 per month or $1,428 per year. The second is up to 200 people for $349 a month or $3,348 per year.

So the best way to determine which one would be right for you is to look at it this way:

- GoToMeeting is perfect for personal or one-on-one coaching.

- GoToWebinar is perfect for large group and business coaching.

- GoToTraining is best for coaches who want an interactive training session online.

You can get a 30-day trial of the "GoTo" suite of products at:

http://internetincomecoach.com/gotowebinar

Next we're going to cover the types of products and services you can offer. Then we'll delve into how you can get clients and talk a bit about taking it to the next level and really getting your business booming!

Chapter 4

Products and Services You Can Offer Your Coaching Clients

The thing to remember when writing your marketing materials is always to focus on the results and benefits, not your own qualifications – and not the actual services and products as much as the perks they deliver.

But once you hook a prospective client into having interest in what you can do for them, you'll want to send them (through a hyperlink) to a place online that describes your products and services in detail. You want to create a program people *want* – not just something *you* enjoy.

We're going to cover coaching services first – and then go into the various things you need to know about creating a line of products online that can offer you residual earnings and free up much of your time to solicit new business and go after big clients without financial hardships.

Personal Coaching Sessions

Many people assume that coaching is just a one size fits all service offering. But in reality, you can customize it to be anything you want. You can do a mix of media formats — audio or video sessions, paired with homework and tutorials.

You can tailor your personal coaching to be as light or in-depth as you want it to be. Your clients will have a variety of needs. Some will need more help than others. Some will be willing to pay for more — while others can only afford the bare bone necessities.

You might tack on email correspondence for questions or issues that arise in between the conversation coaching that the two of your schedule. Let's look at some ideas you can use to create an established individual coaching service plan:

- Various times (30-minute versus 1-hour versus all day versus weekend) — the last two would be beneficial if you hosted an event online similar to a seminar. It's a very "crash course" type of coaching that wouldn't be right for every client (or every coach).

- Access to email correspondence between coaching sessions. You may want to make it limited to a certain number of emails, or unlimited, if you're sure that you won't be overwhelmed with correspondence.

- Specific sessions that you offer. For instance, let's say you're coaching someone on his or her career efforts. You could sell access to various specific sessions such as: Building Confidence for an Interview, Finding a Career That Fits Your Personality, Increasing Your Skillset, Getting the Raise That You Deserve, etc. That way your client could order or pass on whatever sessions they want to.

- You can also have specific training packages that they don't get to choose from. For example, a business might hire you specifically to help one executive transition into the corporation.

This is perfect for coaches who have a set training program or feel confident working with one concept that they can tailor to each individual. If you offer something like this, then you might have prerequisites for your clients.

For example, you couldn't ensure customer satisfaction if you had a program to help someone get an executive position if you allowed a high school dropout working at a minimum wage job sign up for it.

Set reasonable expectations for both yourself and the client. Some coaches will have a 100% money back guarantee if their training and coaching fails to help the client meet his or her objectives. You might want to consider this if your coaching is proven because it will help convert more prospects into clients.

Group Coaching Sessions

Group coaching sessions can be created for personal coaches, but it's most likely going to be used for business purposes. However, if you look at some niches, there are many people who prefer the camaraderie they get when going through this process with others who are struggling.

Think about weekend marriage counseling retreats where there's active couples counseling available in groups – or eating disorder or various addition groups that get coaching together.

Don't rule it out just because you're in the personal coaching business. Consider all of your options. Businesses definitely use group coaching because it lessens the expense they have to endure compared to getting individual sessions for every employee.

Group coaching is great for team building and training. It's also perfect for transitions when new management is coming onboard in a company, or new departments are being set up.

You will see group coaching being done where it's nothing more than a lecture that people attend — and coaching that's very interactive, providing a Question and Answer format during or after the presentation.

Make sure you make good use of surveys and polls when you have a group coaching situation. It's easier to gauge how an individual is progressing, but you will have to pull information out of a group where you're not specifically working one-on-one with anyone.

Publishing an eBook Gives You Instant Authority

As a coach, you have a plethora of tips and thoughts that you share with your clients — or maybe you *wish* you could share. Becoming the author of an eBook not only gives you instant credibility, but it helps brand you in the marketplace.

Most coaches *don't* go the extra mile to do this — and that's one reason why they fail to cement enough clients into their roster. Creating an eBook isn't difficult at all — and it's very inexpensive to list online.

You can create eBooks that you give away for free (used purely for branding purposes and to whet the appetite of your future coaching clients). You can charge a minimal amount like $0.99 and use it as a lead generating tool. Or you can charge more and create a nice passive income for yourself in the process.

An eBook is simply a book that you write using a Word processor online, turn into a PDF file so that people can read it on their computer or electronic gadget, and place for sale or download online where people can access it.

You can even have a ghostwriter (from a site like Elance.com) create an eBook *for* you – where you put your name on it and use it as your own. (You can also edit and tweak it so that it has your own voice if you want to).

Your eBook can be sold or given away directly on your own website or you can list it for sale on a site like Amazon, Barnes and Noble, or ClickBank. If you place it on a site like Amazon or ClickBank, then you can have affiliates promoting your book for you – where you each split the sale.

When you have an eBook, you'll want to hire a professional graphics creator to whip up an eCover for you. It should cost more than $50 to $100 or so – but find one who creates very professional graphics, not a freelancer using a "do it yourself" software that still results in amateur graphics.

Membership Programs Provide Steady Monthly Income

Membership programs are a wonderful residual income source. You can create a series of lessons, upload them to a protected area of your website, and charge a monthly fee for your clients to access them.

Before your launch, you can set up a website that's closed to the public. Create a series of lessons there – text, audio and video media formats. You can either have it set up to drip feed your audience (where they'll get one new lesson each day), or allow them to access it all at once.

You can also set it up where they get monthly access to certain training modules on a schedule by week or by month. Price-wise, you can charge a monthly fee for access, or offer discounts for an annual subscription.

There are tools that will track all of this for you – enrolling members, charging their accounts on autopilot, and blocking them from the system if they cancel their subscription.

Video Courses Are Popular With Today's Clients

Video courses are an alternative to eBooks. Many people prefer learning via video now, and you can provide download access to video tutorials where you give lectures, do screen-captured training sessions, or motivate clients using a video camera.

You can go the extra mile and provide transcripts for your viewing audience if you want to, or provide worksheets for them to download and fill out as they go through the coaching session with you on video.

To house your videos, you can use a service like Amazon S3 where you're only charged according to actual usage. You can set it up to stream to your clients online or download to their PC where they won't have any trouble with Internet speeds.

How to Price Your Products and Services

When pricing your products and services, you want to look at what the marketplace is willing to pay. There will be a wide range – cheaper pricing doesn't always result in more sales.

Sometimes it's the perception of value that gets you more sales. Think of yourself for a minute – if you seriously needed life coaching, would you feel confident with someone who charged $7 an hour?

Or would you feel better about the possibilities of achieving your goals if you met with a coach who charged $150 an hour?

You can definitely start out at a competitive rate, but don't under-value your products and services so much that you cause people to question your value and worth as a coach.

You can coach at a price based on results – although this is very risky. If you're confident enough, you might offer to take a percentage of whatever increase in sales the company achieves during your time spent coaching a team, for example.

You might also charge based on a project instead of hourly. For example, you might be asked to present a bid to help one team transition to a new office or the process or an executive-level transition.

You can obviously up your rates according to certain things, such as:

- Educational achievements (a PhD will charge more than a high school graduate)

- Experience (someone coaching for 20 years commands more than a newcomer)

- Results (someone with ample testimonials has more clout than someone with none)

Some coaches put a simple per hour (or half hour) or per session rate on their website and leave it at that. But you can optimize the services you offer by giving the client the option of purchasing a package deal.

These are done with either monthly packs or based on the number of sessions the person wants to commit to. For example, you can have something that looks like this:

- Individual 1-Hour Coaching: $150

- Monthly Coaching Weekly Package: $480

- Three-Month Coaching Weekly Sessions: $1,440

- Six-Month Coaching Weekly Sessions: $2880

The first rate is your basic hourly session fee that they get when they schedule one coaching session at a time. For the other packages, you could simply take the original fee and give them a 20% discount.

You can adjust this however you want, such as giving them a 5% discount for a monthly package, 10% for a three-month package, and 15% for a six-month package. You can even go with annual discounts. There are no rules on how you offer your pricing.

The great thing is, this gives you a little bit of stability financially – and ensures you won't have to be out scouring for new clients. The client enjoys the perk of a savings when they buy in bulk.

If you find you're having trouble converting prospects into paying clients, then consider offering a free session or a low introductory deal as a way to allow them to experience the coaching you offer.

Then, if they're satisfied with what you helped them accomplish, they can buy one of the regularly priced sessions or coaching packages, depending on what you recommend.

Chapter 5

Securing Clients for Your Coaching Business

After you decide which direction you want to go with your coaching business, get your site set up, and develop your line of products and services, it will be time to work on generating a buzz for your website – getting clients in your virtual doors to find out what you're all about.

We're going to cover 10 ways you can use your branding and marketing materials to secure clients – regardless of whether you're in the personal or business niche market.

We'll go over a variety of online and offline options – because as you'll see, you have the ability to drive traffic to your website (or pull them in) in a bunch of different ways, depending on what you're most comfortable doing.

Getting Your Site Found By Potential Clients Online

There are some things you can do online that help people who are looking for coaching find you. These are people who go to sites like Google or Bing and type in keyword phrases such as, "personal life coach" or "executive business coach," for example.

In order for your site to pop up on those search engines as a possible match for them, you have to have good content online that uses those phrases and conveys to the person that you're the right coach they're looking for.

The first thing you want to do is find out what phrase people type in to find a coach like you. There are free and paid keyword tools that will give you that information.

One free option is the Google Keyword Tool – which is free to use. You can find it by searching Google for "Google Keyword Tool". What you'll do is start with a broad phrase and see what similar ones is comes up with for you. It will also show you how many people are typing that phrase into the search engines.

So for instance, when I type in "business coach" as my starter prompt, I get many results, like this one: "business coaching services" – with 1,000 searches per month. There are 110,000 searches made each month for "career coach," and 60,500 searches for "executive coaching."

Once you do a little keyword research, you'll be able to see *how* people are searching for you online. What you have to do is then create content that tells Google you're the right person they should recommend. Here's how to do that:

First, if you created a static website, you'll want to add a blog to it. A blog will let you create individual posts for each keyword phrase. So you might title one blog entry: *How Does a Career Coach Help You?* And then your blog post would answer that question.

When Google sends traffic to your blog for the keyword phrase career coach, people will be able to see your products and services – and make a decision about whether or not to hire you.

Aside from a blog, you can put articles on article directories like EzineArticles.com. There are many of them available for free, and some paid options. These articles link back to your website in your author's area, so you get branding and backlinks in the process.

Another thing you can do online is look for forums where your products and services might be sought after. For example, let's say you're a personal development coach and one area of expertise is relationship coaching.

You could participate in relationship forums, helping people with their problems. Find a forum that offers the ability to have a signature file – that's an area below each post or comment that you make where you're allowed to have a live hyperlink back to your website.

Whenever you are helpful on a forum, people will be exposed to your link, and if they like what you have to say on the forum, chances are they'll follow the link to your site and buy your products and services.

Social marketing online is another free and easy way to generate traffic to your website. There are several websites where your core audience is hanging out, which include places like:

- Facebook

- Twitter

- Google Plus

- Linked In

There are others, too. For example, if you provide life coaching, then you might be able to use Pinterest and post images (like motivational quotes) that link back to your website.

Or if you are a teen life coach, then you might want to try Instagram or Tumblr, where a younger audience is thriving.

What do you do no these sites? You can create fan pages and groups, engage with your audience, and build a loyal fan base. Let's do one example here:

You could start a Facebook Fan Page or Group for one specific concept, like "Daily Career Motivation" for example. Each day you could post a thought for the day – and it could be a snippet of a blog post that links the reader back to your own website.

Not only do you gain the attention of that person who has "Liked" your Facebook page, but you also get exposure to *their* friends and family – because Facebook is set up now to show a person's activity, so their friends and family will see your post when they Like it or Comment on it – not *only* when they actually Share it.

Network With Other Coaches

Another thing you can do on social networks – and on your own – is to befriend other coaches online and be active on *their* blogs, too. When you have someone come to you who needs coaching, but you realize you're not the right kind of coach they need, do you simply explain that and leave them to go off searching for another solution?

If you befriend other coaches online, then you can all send referral traffic to one another. For example, maybe you're a business coach and you help your client achieve his career goals.

But he's told you there's trouble brewing in his relationship at home. If you have networked your way to success, then you can refer him to a coaching friend of yours who handles relationships.

This is a two-way street — if they're coaching someone for relationships and discover that the person needs career counseling, they can send him to you.

Strategic Partnerships That Boost Your Business

A strategic partnership is different from a coach-to-coach networking situation. With a strategic partner, they're not in the same business as you — but they may be able to send you clients.

In order to make these work, you have to put yourself out there as a viable resource, let people get to know (and trust) you, and be willing to go the extra mile.

Let's look at a situation where you're a career coach and you discover that one of the primary factors driving your client to work with you is the fact that they need more money. They haven't managed what they ear well, so they believe more cash flow will help.

One of the strategic partners you might have is a debt consultant. You would have to have someone you trust — because if you send your client to someone who lacks your ethics, you could be putting them at risk.

Likewise, the debt consultant might see many people who are struggling because they're stuck in a rut with a dead-end career. If a strategic partnership is created, then they can refer people to you as a light at the end of the tunnel that can help them achieve better financial success.

Meet with fellow professionals who you think might make a good match — someone who *also* sees the same kinds of clients as you. Befriend them (truly befriend them) and leave some business cards with them *after* asking them if you can take some of theirs for your clients.

Word of Mouth Referrals

If you're just getting off the ground with your coaching business, then you won't have word of mouth working for you yet. As your business grows and you help people, word of mouth will spread if you do a good job (and unfortunately, also if you don't).

To get things going, you might want to try offering a few people one free session with you. For example, you might find someone in a forum who you know needs help.

You can contact them via private message board and offer to have a Skype session with them once. They'll be grateful and will spread word about your kindness and ethics.

That doesn't mean you'll have a flood of freebie seekers – but it does mean people will see that you have compassion for those in need, and that will make people trust you and want to work with you.

You can also hold a contest – give away one hour-long session to five lucky winners. You can spread the word about this using social media so that it goes viral.

Another way to get word of mouth rolling is to offer perks when people refer other clients to you. You can offer a perk where, if they refer a paying client to you, then they get one free session with you for the month. Depending on your rates, that can be quite a savings.

Speaking Engagements

This is one way you can drive offline traffic to your online business. You have to look at this as part of your marketing process. Begin trying to book speaking engagements at places where your clients will be.

Find listings of events that will have relevant people in attendance. Maybe you're a life coach or business coach specifically for women and you live in the Dallas, Texas area – so you would want to look for something like this on Google:

- "business women event Dallas"

That would show you that there are many events you could try to speak at – such as the Women's Business Conference. You could contact the organizer and offer your services to be a speaker at the event. (At the very least, attend it and network with prospective clients).

You would also see organizations like the Texas Business Women's Association where you would see that they have a weekly meeting. You could attend that meeting and offer to be a speaker at it.

Also check with your Chamber of Commerce, rotary clubs, and things like Kiwanis or Lions Club to see if they know of events where your services would be appreciated.

Direct Sales

Direct sales are never fun – it's hard work- but if you can let your enthusiasm shine through, they *can* pay off for you with some long-term clients and great financial benefits.

Direct sales include cold calling prospective clients, sending out postcards and using direct mail sales copy to convince people that you're something they need for a better life or improved results.

You can hire a professional team or individual to create a script or marketing materials for this specific purpose – or you can do it yourself if you'd feel better about it.

For cold calling, there are lists you can buy from people who have set up lead generation systems to filter names according to those who might be the right match for your business.

Webinars for Groups

We spoke about tools like GoToMeeting and GoToWebinar earlier in this course when we discussed your online alternative to having your own office. That's an option you have to use as a way to get clients, too.

You can schedule webinar events for online prospects where you host a short (30-minute) webinar, take a few Q&A at the end, and generate interest in your products and services.

In this scenario, you might not be contacting a strategic partner in the debt management niche – but you *could* contact a marketer online who is in the credit and debt niche and offer them what's known as a JV partnership.

Many of these marketers have lists of up to 100,000 subscribers or more. So you can make an offer to them that if they will ask their list to attend your webinar, you'll give them a percentage of the sale you get from every client they refer.

Free Workshops and Seminars

Workshops and seminars are offline meeting events that you can host or be a part of in an effort to generate your sales. Look for workshops on college campuses, for example – and see what you could be part of.

There are many colleges that will rent out classrooms or auditoriums where you can host a workshop or seminar and advertise it to the students on campus. You can do the same at some places of business – all you have to do is ask.

Podcasting

A podcast is an audio show that you host on a regular basis (or as you can) and put the file online for a free download via iTunes. You can brand your coaching business and website URL at the beginning and end of your show.

The shows don't have to be lengthy. You can do as much or as little as you like – even 10 minute clips will work, although a common favorite length is between 20-60 minutes.

There are many courses that will walk you through every step of the podcasting process if you choose to use this form of lead generation. Each time you make a new podcast, make sure you share it on your blog and on social networking sites.

Ezine Advertising

An ezine is like an online magazine. It has articles and sometimes ads included in it. Some Ezines even *look* like magazines as far as layout and content – while others are simply email lists where the content you receive is an email from the owner.

There are two ways you can use Ezines – use someone else's, or build your own. There are entire directories out there for other people's Ezines – and you can submit content to them free or for a fee in some cases.

It's similar to how an article directory works – you create content, have an author's bio box with a hyperlink back to your website, and you submit the content and wait for it to go live.

Only in this case, you submit content for a free spot or you buy space in an upcoming issue for your article and it gets emailed out to the ezine owner's list of subscribers, which can sometimes be over 100,000 individuals.

The flip side of this is to launch your *own* free ezine. For this, you'll need to build a list. There are some free tools that allow this (like MailChimp), but then you're limited to how many subscribers you can have – and you have intrusive ads showing up in your emailed Ezines.

A better option would be to invest in a tool like Aweber. They offer a $1 one month trial and then it starts at $19.95 a month for the first 10,000 subscribers. You'll go through the step-by-step process of setting up your "opt in form" which is where they enter their name and email address on your blog or site to get signed up.

Once it's all in place, you'll be ready to create a series of ezine issues to go out to your audience. If you're not a good writer, then you may want to come up with a few topics, have a freelancing ghostwriter create the content, and then just tweak it so that it has your voice and whatever message you want it to have.

You'll be able to drip your issues out to each new subscriber that comes along using a Follow Up email system – all on autopilot. Try to create evergreen content that won't get outdated. But they do have options for more timely communications, too.

Once you have an ezine system in place, you can send out a Broadcast email to announce things like an upcoming webinar, a new book release, or even openings in your schedule to accept new coaching clients.

All of these techniques in this chapter will work for you regardless of what target audience you're going after. Look into each of them and fully implement it to see how it works to convert prospects into paying customers for you. You might find that some strategies work better than others.

Next, we're going to look at how you take an online coaching business to the next level. How can you stabilize the income and achieve greater financial rewards?

Chapter 6

Taking Your Coaching Business to the Next Level

We've already discussed your ability to add a product line of things like eBooks and CD or video courses to increase residual earnings from your coaching business online.

But let's look at a few ways you can up your fees and position yourself to be one of the most sought after coaches in your niche market.

Performance or Results Fees

When you get to a level where your client roster is full and your business is thriving – and you've maxed out a good hourly pay wage – you can switch to a different pay scale and possibly make more money.

This primarily works best for business coaches, but it could also benefit a personal coach whose focus was on income gains or financial stability for an individual or couple.

Instead of charging an hourly wage (or in addition to a lower hourly wage), what you do is have a fee based on a guarantee of results through your performance as a coach.

There has to be parameters set. You can't just say, "If I help you find a better job, I am paid a fee of X amount..." Let's say you have a client who currently earns $85,000. He wants a six-figure salary.

You agree to coach him to a job where he earns that figure. The difference is $15,000 in salary for him. Your agreement might say that you are to be paid 25% of the increase in salary, which would be $3,750.

Now if you're charging a $150 hourly wage, and you think it would take less than 25 coaching sessions to get this person to the next level, then it will increase your pay wage.

You want to analyze each person on a case-by-case basis – because if they don't hold up *their* end of the bargain, it could be a waste of time for you – and lost income.

Many companies will pay per project or for performance. If you're good enough, and confident enough in your abilities, then this may be a route you want to go. You have to find a balance between charging enough and too much.

Companies won't just be looking for bottom line fees — they want results, so if you have the experience to command more money, don't be afraid to ask for it — especially if you have testimonials to back you up.

Long-Term Clients

Some coaches see a client as a short-term income stream. They have certain programs set up that they go through which only take a limited period of time. But as you get more experience with your coaching business, you may want to focus on preparing a long-term strategy that keeps your client onboard for an unlimited timespan.

Coaching can last for years, not just weeks or months. If you compare fledgling coaches with extremely successful ones, you'll see that those who are thriving have long relationships with their clients.

Self-development isn't about reaching one goal and being done. It's about always bettering yourself. You can always find things to work with your client on — because even at their very best, there's always some way life can be even better.

Don't wait for your client to devise a long-term plan. You need to make one for them, present it and keep them signed up with you continually. So if someone comes in to work on career stuff, you can work with them to achieve that goal – but then make sure you end with a lead-in to the rest of their life – topics like:

- Relationships – with spouse, kids, friends and family

- Physical Health – such as weight, energy levels, etc.

- Mental Health – stress relief, depression, anxiety

Go down the list of all the things you could work with them on and dig into it a little bit. Some of this may come out during sessions for the original goal. For example, let's say a client comes to you to help them get a better career.

In passing, they might mention that their wife is always browbeating them to be more successful. Jot a note down about this – it means there's a crack in the relationship that can be explored later.

When you start acquiring a long list of long-term clients, rather than short-term ones, it will ease the continual marketing burden you have to keep pulling in new business.

Become an In-Demand Speaker or a Top Notch Author

We talked about speaking engagements and creating eBooks earlier in the course, but this is something I want to stress – because working on this (even if you're not a "speaker" or "author" by trade) could really catapult you to the next level of success.

Once you work on your own book – and perhaps set it up in Amazon Kindle and on Amazon as a print on demand publication – you suddenly achieve a certain amount of authority associated with your name.

You'll want to release a press release about it and make yourself available for interviews by trade magazines and other publications – even television segments!

Learn all you can about writing a book and then bypass the traditional publishing houses that take years to launch it – do it yourself online and gain instant credibility.

If you're not comfortable speaking in front of a large crowd, then start off with a YouTube audience. You can reach just as many (if not more) people, but you have the ability to edit the speech to your liking.

Once you add the "author" and "speaker" titles to your usual coaching one, you'll be able to charge much more –

whether you're using an hourly/per session/per project rate or charging a fee based on performance and results.

License Your Program for Other Coaches to Use

Have you developed a specific coaching system or program that you take people through? This could be used for personal or business coaching – either one. If you do, then you might consider having a certification or licensing program where other coaches can benefit from your knowledge.

There are many coaches out there who get trained on Tony Robbins coaching – they're *coached* on how to coach! You can do that as well. Other coaches who are struggling or new to the business may jump at the chance to be able to use your program to help their clients.

You can charge fees for certifying people and allowing them to use your materials. Some programs make people get re-certified each year, or pay a monthly or annual membership program fee to use the materials.

You can have different levels of certification, too. Don't think that because you're new, you can't launch a program like this – if the content is good, it's worth sharing with others!

Starting your own online coaching business can be very exhilarating. It takes work and dedication to the branding process, but once you start building a loyal fan base, you'll enjoy the financial and other perks that come with being an online entrepreneur.

Resources

The following are my recommended resources at the time of printing of this book. You can always access my most up-to-date recommended resources at:

InternetIncomeCoach.com/resources

Wordpress: I recommend building your coaching website / blog using the Wordpress platform. Most good web hosting companies will allow you to install Wordpress free on your hosting account.

HostGator: For hosting your coaching website and blog, I recommend using HostGator. As mentioned above; you can install the Wordpress platform free on a HostGator hosting account. Use coupon code "incomecoach25" at HostGator.com to save 25% off your order of any new hosting account.

Skype: When doing 1 on 1 coaching calls with international clients, Skype of my go to choice. You can download Skype free at: Skype.com.

GoToWebinar: For doing group coaching and training my favorite tool is GoToWebinar by Citrix. You can read my review of GoToWebinar and get a 30 day free trial at:

InternetIncomeCoach.com/gtw

WishList Member: If you are interested in creating an online membership program for your coaching or group coaching clients, I highly recommend using WishList Memember, which integrates with your Wordpress site to give it membership functionality. You can learn more about WishList Member at:

InternetIncomeCoach.com/wishlistmember

NameCheap: When it comes to domain names, most people are familiar with GoDaddy. For reasons I won't get into here, I personally use and recommend NameCheap to buy my domain names. You can learn more about NameCheap at:

InternetIncomeCoach.com/namecheap

About the Author

Brian T. Edmondson is an author, speaker, and Internet entrepreneur who helps website owners get more traffic, build their email lists, and increase sales online.

After leaving his "Wall Street" job in 2001, Brian found true success and independence through the power of the Internet, which he believes offers the greatest entrepreneurial opportunity in history.

Brian has worked with and consulted many of the world's top online companies and entrepreneurs including Agora Publishing, Early to Rise, The Learning

Annex, American Writer's & Artists, Michael Masterson, and MaryEllen Tribby.

He truly lives the "internet lifestyle", working full time online from his home outside of Philadelphia, PA (or anywhere he can get his MacBook Air connected to the internet).

You can learn more about Brian and download a free copy of his special report, *The Internet Profit Report*, at InternetIncomeCoach.com and connect with him on Facebook at Facebook.com/InternetIncomeCoach.

Made in the USA
Middletown, DE
15 May 2016